SUPER
QUICK
SKILLS

Build Your Argument

Dave
Rush

Los Angeles | London | New Delhi
Singapore | Washington DC | Melbourne

Los Angeles | London | New Delhi
Singapore | Washington DC | Melbourne

SAGE Publications Ltd
1 Oliver's Yard
55 City Road
London EC1Y 1SP

SAGE Publications Inc.
2455 Teller Road
Thousand Oaks, California 91320

SAGE Publications India Pvt Ltd
B 1/I 1 Mohan Cooperative Industrial Area
Mathura Road
New Delhi 110 044

SAGE Publications Asia-Pacific Pte Ltd
3 Church Street
#10-04 Samsung Hub
Singapore 049483

Editor: Jai Seaman
Assistant editor: Charlotte Bush
Production editor: Ian Antcliff
Marketing manager: Catherine Slinn
Cover design: Shaun Mercier
Typeset by: C&M Digitals (P) Ltd, Chennai, India
Printed in the UK

Library of Congress Control Number: 2020941408

British Library Cataloguing in Publication data

A catalogue record for this book is available from the
British Library

ISBN 978-1-5297-5210-6

At SAGE we take sustainability seriously. Most of our products are printed in the UK using responsibly
sourced papers and boards. When we print overseas we ensure sustainable papers are used as measured
by the PREPS grading system. We undertake an annual audit to monitor our sustainability.

Contents

Everything in this book!

Section 1   What is an argument?

Before you can start to build your own arguments, you need to understand what one is in an academic context, and what your lecturers are looking for.

Section 2   Where do I start?

Getting going can be one of the most difficult steps, and it's vital that you start off by understanding your question, and your purpose.

Section 3   How do I generate ideas?

Gather the blocks you will use to construct your argument, and make sure that you are including all the necessary content.

Section 4   What is MY argument?

Use your ideas to decide exactly what your answer is before you start planning.

Section 5 How do I structure my argument?

Now you have your answer you can start to organise your materials into a clear structure for taking your reader there.

Section 6 How do I support my argument?

Every point in your argument has to be backed up with appropriate evidence, and you need to make sure that you are engaging with that evidence properly.

Section 7 How do I deal with counter arguments?

Showing your awareness of other points of view and their limitations will make your own argument much stronger, and demonstrate that you've taken into account what other experts have to say.

Section 8 How do I write a good argument?

You've done the thinking, but now you need to get it down on paper, clearly, concisely, and always sticking to the point.

Section 9 What makes a killer conclusion?

Writing a good conclusion is one of the most important elements in making sure your argument has the most impact – and gets the best marks.

Section 10 How do I do better next time?

Every time you build an argument, you should reflect on your experience to see how you can do better next time, and set realistic and achievable goals for the future.

What is an argument?

10 second
summary

An argument is a position taken in
response to a question, and supported
by propositions or reasons why that
position is true, or convincing.

60 second summary

An argument is both your overall answer/position, and all the steps that you go through to reach that position. That means when lecturers talk about 'your argument' they mean both your final destination, and how you got there. They expect your argument to be supported by evidence at every stage, and to always reach a clear conclusion.

Arguments are a key feature of all types of academic writing, and academic thought. They are most obvious in essays in the humanities and social sciences, but also appear in other forms that may at first glance appear more descriptive or purely factual. So whether it is in a research report, a presentation, or in a seminar discussion, the ability to form a clear and valid argument is a vital academic skill.

Types of argument

Arguments come in lots of different forms, and the type you need to build will depend on the subject you are studying, and the type of question you are answering, or task you are carrying out.

> 'Arguments are only needed when more than one answer is possible. Facts are not arguments, but arguments arise when we need to say what facts mean.'

Broadly speaking, there are two main types of argument that you will need to build during your studies. These are the explanatory, and the discursive. In practice, most tasks involve a combination of the two, in different ratios.

1   **Explanatory arguments** are not just descriptions, but are what you need when you are asked to explain something: either *why* something happened the way that it did, *how* something works or is put together, or *what* would happen in a particular set of circumstances.

2   **Discursive arguments** are about considering all of the different possible ways of looking at something, whether that be a set of data, or a particular issue. The word 'discursive' is related to the word 'discuss', which you will see in a lot of essay questions, particularly in the humanities, but it applies to any argument that is trying to provide an objective account of a range of possible positions.

Discursive arguments can also be *evaluative*, where you are weighing up the strengths and weaknesses or efficacy of something, or *comparative*, where you are making judgements about how different positions relate and differ. They can also be *analytical*, where you are taking something apart and examining every piece, and seeing how they all relate and contribute to the whole.

A student told us

'I don't understand what my lecturer means when they say I need to be critical.'

Being **critical** in an academic context is not the same as being critical elsewhere, where it is often used to describe being negative about something. Criticality at university is about questioning, about not taking anything at face value, and about making judgements about the value of something. These can just as easily be positive judgements as negative ones.

How do I build different arguments?

In order to build an argument yourself, it is important to know that arguments can be put together in very different ways. The following are some ways that you can think about common types of argument and how they are built.

The pillars and roof

In some cases you will have multiple different propositions that all support an overall position. These propositions are related to, but not dependent on, each other. Think of it like a set of pillars holding up a roof, where the roof is your answer, and the pillars are the reasons that support it.

Feminism is the most important movement of the twentieth century.

Feminism achieved a wide range of political and social changes globally in the twentieth century.

Feminism inspired other movements and worked closely with them.

Feminist theory was central in understanding that gender, and other, identities are socially constructed and not 'natural'.

The logic chain

In other arguments you need to show how each proposition relates to the next, and how that all leads to the inevitable conclusion: your answer. Think of this like a chain, or mathematical equation, where each point is linked together by a logic word – so, and, therefore, but – and so on.

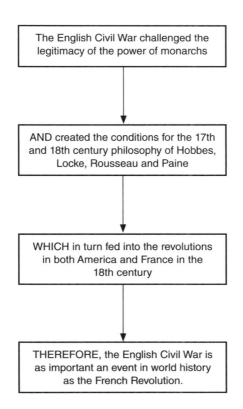

The English Civil War challenged the legitimacy of the power of monarchs

AND created the conditions for the 17th and 18th century philosophy of Hobbes, Locke, Rousseau and Paine

WHICH in turn fed into the revolutions in both America and France in the 18th century

THEREFORE, the English Civil War is as important an event in world history as the French Revolution.

The straight fight

Sometimes you will need to set two points of view against each other, and look at which is most convincing. Here, you will have an argument (or thesis), a counterargument (or antithesis) and a synthesis, where you bring together the discussion of the two sides and show what your position is. Often this will be a combination of elements from the two sides, with something of your own thrown in.

Thesis statement A short summary of exactly what your argument is about. Basically, this is your answer in a nutshell.

Synthesis Bringing together different views in order to form an overall position that combines them all.

Example:

Thesis: Racial equality is guaranteed by law, therefore racial equality has been achieved in the UK.

Antithesis: Statistics including arrest rates, representation in political and business positions, and educational attainment gaps show that racial inequality still exists in the UK.

Synthesis: Equality is created not just through legislation, but through social, institutional and cultural factors.

Conclusion: Racial equality is not a reality in the UK.

As well as thinking about what an argument *is*, it's also important to think about what an argument *is not*, and so avoid some common mistakes. Circle the correct answers below.

An argument is:

1   Objective...yes/no

2   Like an argument in everyday life.....................................yes/no

3   A list...yes/no

4   An opportunity to show how much you know
    about a topic or subject...yes/no

Answers:

1   Yes. An argument is based on evidence, not opinion, emotion, or belief.

2   No. It is not necessarily about disagreeing, or yes versus no. This is about using evidence and reviewing existing positions in order to decide your answer to a question and explain your reasoning.

3   No. 'Here's ten things I noticed about Hamlet' or 'three strengths of capitalism and three weaknesses' is not an argument, it is a set of bullet points.

4   No. Every point you include must be relevant, and in the service of your overall position.

Where do I start?

10 second
summary

Before you do anything else, it is
vital that you understand what you
are trying to achieve.

You need to understand your question (if you have one), and more importantly, what your purpose is. Throughout this book, we will focus on responding to questions, as this is the most common place you will need to build arguments, whether in writing, in presentations, or in discussion with others. However, everything that we think about here is relevant to any time that you build an argument, whether at university or in your life beyond.

The key thing here is to think about not just your argument, but the *context* in which it is taking place. If you understand *why* you are arguing something, you are much more likely to make a good job of it.

Take a look at the following questions. These are all taken from real modules at undergraduate level. Underline what you think are the key words or phrases, and take a few notes on why these terms are important, and what they tell you.

Question 1: Feminism is the most important movement of the twentieth century. Discuss.

Question 2: The English Civil War is as important an event in world history as the French Revolution. Discuss.

Question 3: What is the House of Lords, and to what extent does it still symbolise a British 'class' system?

What do the key words or phrases tell you?

....

....

....

....

....

....

When analysing a question, there are three important factors to consider: the **instruction**, the **topic** and the **limit**.

In questions 1 and 2, the **instruction** is the same: 'discuss'. This tells you that you're being asked to construct a *discursive argument*, and to examine the possible points of view on a position. In question 1, the **topic** is feminism, but this question is not just asking you to discuss this in general, but to talk about feminism's importance as a movement in the twentieth century. That is your **limit** – in other words, the part of the topic you need to talk about. You should only include content relevant to that limit.

In question 2, you're being asked to compare (**instruction**) the English Civil War and the French Revolution (**topic**), but only in terms of their importance to world history (**limit**). You do not need to give any detail about either event other than what is necessary to discuss this particular issue.

In question 3, there two elements to the **instruction**, with both an *explanatory* element (What is...?) and a *discursive* element (to what extent...?). The **topic** is the House of Lords, but again, only in terms of its status as symbolic of the class system (**limit**).

> 'The most common mistake that students make is writing about the topic, but not answering the question.'

Recognising, and sticking to these limits is really important at university. At school it can be enough to demonstrate that you understand the basic facts of a situation, or that you know a certain amount about a topic. At university, that is a given, and what is important is showing that you have the ability to think critically about those facts and the different possible interpretations of them. If you discuss things outside the scope of the question, no matter how relevant they are to the topic, then you are both not gaining any marks, and wasting words that you could be using to talk about things that are important.

A student told us

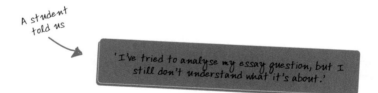

> 'I've tried to analyse my essay question, but I still don't understand what it's about.'

If you are having trouble working out what a question is asking you, you can also try and rephrase it, to see if that helps. For example, question 2 above could become 'Why do some people argue that the English Civil War is less important to world history than the French Revolution? Are they right?' Rephrasing a question can also be a useful way to help you generate more ideas, which we will look at in Section 3.

Understanding your purpose

Once you have thought about your question, you also need to think about not just what you are doing, but why you are doing it.

Whenever you are starting to think about an argument, or a task, ask yourself the following questions.

Why is this question important?

Remember that one of the key purposes of all assessment at university is to show your lecturers what you have learnt from them – so make sure to relate your argument to what's been discussed on the relevant module or course. Why has your lecturer set this question? Why this question and not another?

If you are coming up with your own question, or building an argument from scratch, then ask yourself – why does this matter? What is important, or interesting, about this topic or issue? In other words, if someone asked you, 'So what?', what would you say?

What do I need to demonstrate?

All assessments at university are designed to test both your knowledge and your ability to carry out certain tasks. Make sure to think about both what **content** you need to include, but also what **skills** you need to show you have mastered.

What can the instructions tell me?

It is really important that you focus not just on the question, but also on any other instructions you have been given. They are there for a reason. For example, the word limit, or time length, is part of the task – you need to be able to argue your case in the space provided.

How does this fit into my studies as a whole?

Is this a self-contained task, or a task that is designed to help you do something else? For example, writing a literature review is an important skill in its own right, but also an exercise that lecturers set to help prepare you to do pieces of independent research.

Does this relate to a broader life skill?

All academic tasks train you in certain skills that will be useful in life. Make sure that everything you do is as useful as possible by thinking about what this task is teaching you; whether that be synthesising information, analysing data, or building an argument.

CHECK POINT

Have you:

☐ Read and analysed the question in detail?

☐ Read all other instructions and understood them?

☐ Understood why you have been set this task and what you are expected to demonstrate?

If the answer to any of the above is 'no', and you are feeling stuck, ask one of your tutors, or a fellow student. Don't suffer in silence!

How do I generate ideas?

10 second
summary

Before you do anything else, you
need to think about what you already
know, and what more you might
need to find out.

It is common to either have an immediate, almost instinctive response to a question (the 'I know the answer to this!' response), or to have absolutely no idea what to say (the 'I'm going to fail!' response). Either way, you need to think about all the ideas you have, and everything that might relate to your argument BEFORE you come up with an answer. It's important to do this, as otherwise *confirmation bias* could lead you to focus on everything that agrees with your first response, and ignore other possibilities.

Taking the time to do this properly is really important, as it will make life much easier later on, and will help you to deal with anxiety and procrastination.

Self-reflection

Before going any further, take **five minutes** to think about the following. The last time you had to come up with an argument, what process did you go through? What steps did you take, and how well did it go? Note your thoughts below.

Be honest with yourself, both about what went well, and what could have gone better.

....

....

....

....

....

....

'There is no such thing as a perfect student, or a perfect way of doing things. You need to find out what works for you.'

Where do I get my ideas from?

Once you have analysed your question and thought about your purpose, you need to see what you already know. Think about the following:

- Are there particular lectures, or topics that you have covered, that are relevant to the question?

- Can you make any connections with other topics or things you've learnt?

- What have you read that might be relevant? Is there anything on your reading lists that you haven't read yet that looks useful?

- Have you had any discussions, either in class, with a lecturer, or elsewhere, that might help?

- Is there an existing debate about this topic? Has your lecturer mentioned anything that they might expect you to refer to in your argument?

- What possible answers and arguments can you think of? Try to think not just of answers you agree with, but *any possible answer*. This is a good mental exercise, and will also help you to anticipate counter arguments.

- What is the overall module/course about? Are there particular learning objectives that are being tested by this task? Most courses and modules list these objectives, so if you're not sure what they are, go and check in the course details, or ask your lecturer.

- Are there any obvious gaps in your knowledge? Is there a part of the question that you know much less about? Is any extra research needed?

You need to take notes on your responses to all of these questions, and it's really important that before you do any extra research, you make sure that you cover everything your lecturers have directed you towards. Remember – you are being tested on what you have learnt from them, as well as on what you can find out for yourself.

How do I record my ideas?

The most important thing at this stage is to make sure that no ideas are lost, and that you are getting things down in a way that will be helpful to you in the rest of the process. There are lots of ways that you can take notes, and record ideas. The following are just some examples, and you need to think honestly about what works for you, and why.

Notes – The most simple way is just to write down continuous notes. You can do this by hand, or online. Try and keep them brief and to the point.

Cornell style notes – This is a common form of notetaking, which involves leaving a wide margin down the left-hand side of the page which you can use as you go, or when reviewing, to add subtitles and comments.

Sticky notes – Writing points or ideas on individual sticky notes can be really useful, and can allow you to move things around and make connections between your ideas. There are lots of apps that you can use to do this virtually, such as Padlet.

Mind map – This is a more visual way of taking notes in the form of a diagram, and can help to group ideas and points together. Again, there are lots of apps that will help you to do this, or you can just do it by hand.

Audio recording – Some people find it much easier to record notes and ideas verbally. If you find information easier to process when listening than when reading, this could be worth a try. Talk-to-text software can be really useful here.

'The most important thing I learnt was not to just go through old notes, or what I'd read, with a highlighter. I could never find anything when I needed it later, and writing points out again made me really think about and engage with them.'

Tip

Make sure that any direct quotations that you've included in your notes are clearly marked, so that you don't accidentally commit plagiarism. Also make sure to be clear where every idea has come from, so that you don't have to go hunting back through all your materials later on.

CHECK POINT

Have you:

- Reflected on what you do well, and what you could improve?

- Looked at all relevant notes and course materials?

- Chosen a note-taking method that suits the task and your own preferences?

- Clearly noted where all your ideas have come from?

What is MY argument?

10 second
summary

In order to plan your route, you need to know where you're going. Let's think about how you work out your overall answer.

Before working on a plan, you must have a clear sense of what it is that you want to argue. It is a common mistake to start trying to organise your ideas into a structure without really knowing what your overall position is, which leads to arguments that are woolly and confusing.

It is also important that you are able to give your answer concisely and clearly. The issues that you discuss at university are complex and difficult, and it can be tempting to tell yourself that your answer is too complicated to sum up quickly. That is not true, and if you can't sum it up quickly, the chances are you haven't understood it properly.

'I get intimidated by the idea that I'm supposed
to come up with something new, or original. I'm
only a first year!'

In university mark schemes you will often see reference to 'originality' or 'critical thought', and your lecturers will sometimes say that you need to include your 'own opinion'. All of these terms can be scary, or confusing.

Remember, you are not expected to come up with something entirely new, or something that no-one has ever thought of before. You just need to demonstrate your ability to think about what other people have said and question, compare, evaluate, analyse – basically, show that you have done some thinking about what you've learned and the research you've done – and that you're not just repeating what is already there.

Equally, to talk about giving 'your opinion' in an academic context is misleading. An 'opinion' is subjective and can be based on emotion or belief. The important word is *your* – what your lecturers want to see is *your* position, and how *you* support that position with evidence and reasoning.

Thesis statements

You will sometimes see your overall argument referred to as a *thesis statement*. This sounds complicated, but it isn't. A 'thesis' is an idea or theory that is put forward to be tested or proved, so a 'thesis statement' is just a way of talking about what your overall answer or argument is going to be.

Coming up with a thesis statement is a useful way of checking that you have a clear idea of what you are trying to say, and is really helpful in preparing introductions and conclusions, or explaining your ideas to other people.

Because your thesis statement is going to encapsulate your whole argument, it needs to cover both your final answer, and some of the key reasons supporting that answer.

It is good to keep thesis statements as short as possible and, wherever possible, to just one sentence.

For example:

> *The House of Lords has less political power than it used to, but the fact that an unelected body containing aristocrats, wealthy businessmen and members of the clergy still has such prominence makes it highly symbolic of the continuing importance of the class system in Britain.*

Or

> *Feminism is the most important movement of the twentieth century, because of the numerous political and social achievements it motivated, and because it popularised the idea that identities are socially constructed, and not 'natural', and so can be challenged, and changed.*

Note how in each case I have incorporated key terms from the titles into the thesis statement. This is a good way of making sure that you are answering the question, and not straying off topic.

Now it's your turn. If you are working on an assignment at the moment, then take ten minutes to look over your notes. If not, then find an example question, and take ten minutes to make some notes about it. Then, do the following:

Step 1: Take five minutes to write notes about what your answer is. Try and write at least 100 words, if you can. These can be full sentences and paragraphs, but they don't have to be. Notes are fine.

....

....

....

....

....

....

....

....

....

Step 2: Take three minutes to condense these notes into one sentence. It might help you to start with, 'This essay will argue that' (or 'This presentation', or just 'I').

....

....

....

TIP

If you are finding it difficult to come up with an answer then try writing several different thesis statements. Sometimes pretending that you are going to argue in a particular way will help you to realise what it is that you actually want to say.

CHECK
POINT

Summing ideas up in one sentence is a good way of checking your understanding of ideas, and remembering them for the future. It can really help you see if you've developed a clear end point for your argument, as you've just done, but it is also a useful skill in many other areas of study.

To practise doing this, see if you can write a definition of a thesis statement in one sentence.

A thesis statement is....

....

....

....

....

....

Congratulations!

You have now come up with your overall argument. In some ways this is the most difficult step, and a clear idea of what you want to say is the most important part of building any argument.

How do I structure my argument?

10 second
summary

Now you have your answer you can
start to organise all your materials
and build the structure that will
support your overall position.

There is no magic recipe book of structures, and no one right way of structuring any argument. What you want to argue should determine how you go about building your argument – but there are some common frameworks and approaches that can help you.

Writing a strong plan is a really important part of building any argument. Having a clear end point is vital, but if you want to make your argument convincing you need the path to that point to be as clear and easy to follow as possible.

> 'Your plan is your map, and like any journey, if you set off without good directions it is easy to get lost.'

Building a plan

It helps to break the task of structuring your argument into two parts. First, you need to come up with a brief skeleton, which gives you an outline of the steps that you will take, which we will look at in this section. Second, you need to flesh out that skeleton, and turn the outline into a full picture, by working out exactly what you will include, and why. We will look at this process in Section 6.

Writing an outline

Take a couple of minutes to analyse the following presentation question. As outlined in Section 2, think about the **instruction**, the **topic**, and the **limit**.

Equality is guaranteed by law in the UK – but has racial equality been achieved in reality?

Instruction...

....

Topic...

....

Limit...

....

Now look at the following points from a student's notes. Is there any way that these could be grouped together in order to help you create an outline? What connections can you think of, and do any of the points support more than one argument?

1. The Equality Act 2010 = illegal to discriminate on the basis of race.

2. The 2019 parliament has highest proportion of BAME MPs in UK history (c.10%).

3. 26% of white Britons said they were prejudiced against people of other races in 2017.

4. 7.4% of board members at FTSE100 companies BAME in 2019.

5. Prominent people of colour in wide variety of cultural areas, esp. music and sport.

6. 14% of UK population from an ethnic minority.

7. Racist attacks increased since 2016 Brexit vote.

Before we look at how we could start to build an outline from these points, think about the following questions:

- Does the question suggest a structure?

- Does rephrasing the question help?

- What is your overall argument going to be?

The 'block' structure

Here, we can see that a basic structure is suggested, because at its most simple, this is a yes/no question ('Has racial equality been achieved in the UK?'). Therefore, we could have something like the 'straight fight' structure from Section 1, with all the points to suggest that racial equality has been achieved in one section (yes), and all the points to suggest that it hasn't in another (no). Sometimes you will see this referred to as a 'block' structure.

For this structure, points 1, 2 and 5 could go on the 'yes' side, with points 3, 4 and 7 on the 'no' side. Point 6 is usable on either.

YES	NO
1, 2, 5	3, 4, 7
(6)	

The 'point by point' structure

However, this is not the only way of grouping these points. You can also link them by the area they relate to. For example, points 1, 2, and 4 could be grouped under the heading 'Political and economic', while points 3 and 5 could be grouped as 'Social and cultural'. Point 7 could fall into either grouping, while 6, again, is usable anywhere.

Political/economic	Social/cultural
1, 2, 4	3, 5
(6) (7)	

Turning it from a list into an argument

We have now grouped our points together, but we still do not have a clear idea of how they form an argument. This is a more ordered list than the notes at the beginning, but it is still just a list.

The next stage is to think about how we are going to order these points, and link them together to form the skeleton of an argument. To do this, we also need to decide our answer. For this example, I am going to use the following thesis statement:

This presentation will argue that despite some improvements, racial equality is still not a reality in the UK.

Let's see how we can use our block and point by point structures to get us to this endpoint.

Which comes first, the yes or the no?

The first thing we need to decide is which order our sections will go in. As we are going to argue 'No', it makes sense that the 'No' section comes last, before our conclusion, as this means that we can address any arguments raised in the first half in the second, to make things less confusing for the reader.

That gives us the following two possible outlines.

Block

YES:

- Racial equality protected by law (1)

- More prominent people of colour across many areas of UK culture and society (5)

- Current UK government most ethnically diverse ever, with c.10% BAME MPs (2).

HOWEVER

NO:

- 14% UK population from an ethnic minority background (6) = parliament still not representative

- Business the same → only 7.4% BAME board members (4)

- 26% admit prejudice (3)

- Brexit vote → increasing no. racist attacks (7).

Point by point

Political and economic

YES:

- Racial equality protected by law (1).

HOWEVER

NO:

- 14% UK population from an ethnic minority background (6)
- Representation in parliament (2) and business (4) = political and economic equality still not reality.

Social and cultural

YES:

- Likewise, more prominent people of colour across many areas of UK culture and society (5).

HOWEVER

NO:

- 26% admit to prejudice (3) and Brexit vote → increasing no. racist attacks (7).

This is a simplified version of the process, and other types of structure are possible. 'Block' and 'point by point' structures work well for yes/no, evaluative, and 'discuss' questions where you are given a position and asked to explore its validity, but these structures also work well for explanatory arguments, where the two blocks can be differing versions of *why* or *what*, or the factors in an explanation can be explored point by point.

The key is that whatever structure you end up with, this is a process that helps you turn a mass of unstructured information (your notes and ideas) into a clear and focused line of argument.

A student
told us

'I never have time to plan an essay properly – the deadline is always too close.'

Spending a long time writing a plan is not 'wasting time' that could be better spent on writing. The more time you spend planning, the less time it will take you to produce your final argument, as you will already have put in the hard work of thinking everything through. This is a really important part of testing that your argument works – your plan is like a dress rehearsal where you make sure everything works.

Using a thesis statement and a few supporting points from an assignment on your course, have a go at creating a block structure.

Your thesis statement:

Supporting points:

1

2

3

4

Yes:

–

–

However, no:

–

–

How do I support my argument?

10 second summary

In order to make your argument convincing, it needs to be well supported at every step.

To make sure your argument is fully supported at every stage, you need to make a properly detailed plan. An outline is a good start, and helps work out the basic steps you will take, but you also need to look at exactly where all of your points and ideas will go, and how they will link together.

You also need to make sure that every point you make is supported with evidence. To do this, you need evidence that is appropriate for an academic context, and to use it in the correct way.

Fleshing out the skeleton

Now that you have your outline, you need to return to your notes and work out where all the pieces will go. You may already have begun this when generating ideas. But whether you've done a lot, or a little, the following actions could help make sure that you get everything in the right place.

Coding

Go through your notes and mark everything with a 'code' that shows you where it needs to go. This code can be as simple or as complicated as you like – for example, it could just be a 'Y' or an 'N', to signify which side of the argument a point supports, or it could be a letter or number to show which section the point should go in.

Tip

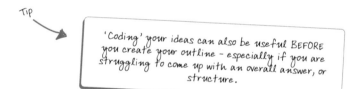

'Coding' your ideas can also be useful BEFORE you create your outline – especially if you are struggling to come up with an overall answer, or structure.

What makes the cut?

Next, you need to think about what goes in, and what you don't have space for. Most of the time you will have far more material than you are able to include, and it can be difficult to decide what to leave out.

One way to approach this is to grade each point regarding its importance to the overall argument. In other words, what *has* to go in? What does the argument absolutely rely on? What is interesting, and relevant, but not vital? What is interesting, but perhaps not entirely relevant? And so on.

As you go through and 'code' your notes, highlight the points that you think are key. These should be the first that you add into your structure. Then you can work your way through the rest of your points from the most important down to the least, and slot them in one by one. You'll soon realise when you are running out of space...

Remember, it's important that any material from another source is there to back up something that you want to say, and must be fully relevant to the question at hand, and not just the broader topic. Don't include something unless it is doing something in your argument.

> 'Evidence should be there to support your argument, not be your argument.'

Are there any gaps?

As you go through the process of giving each point a place in the structure, you will start to see if there are any gaps. If there are, you need to do the following:

- Revisit your course materials. Have you missed anything?

- Look at your reading lists, and other texts referenced by your lecturers. Does anything look useful?

- Do some independent research. Start in the library, and if you're going to use the internet, make sure that you're only using reliable sources.

Assessing your evidence

Whether you are doing independent research, or drawing on sources that you've been directed to, you have to ensure that everything you use in your argument is appropriate for university study. Let's look at some common sources of evidence, and whether it's okay to use them.

Wikipedia

No… and yes. A lot of students have it drummed into them that Wikipedia is not an acceptable source, because it can be edited by anyone. However, the fundamental problem with Wikipedia is not actually the *reliability* of the information (which is normally good), it is that it is *too basic*. Wikipedia, as the name suggests, is an online encyclopedia – it is there to give simple, background information. At university level, that is not enough. Websites such as Wikipedia can be a good place to start when you don't know anything about a topic, but it shouldn't ever be what makes it into your final argument.

Academic journal articles

Yes. Academic journals and books are the key resource for university study. They are where lecturers and academics publish their research. This should be where the majority of your evidence comes from.

Newspaper articles

Sometimes. Newspaper articles are sometimes the only sources available to you; for example, if you are looking at prevailing social opinions, or very recent events. They must, however, be treated with caution as they can be biased, and they are often quite basic.

Books

Sometimes. Books from academic publishers are usually fine, but not all books are as reliable. As with websites, anyone can produce or publish a book, and many are either not of the required standard, or not balanced.

The key things that you need to think about when assessing the material you are using to support your argument, then, is whether the source has the requisite **credibility** and **complexity**. You should only be using material that can be trusted to be objective, and that is at the right level of difficulty.

A student told us

'I don't understand what makes a book or an article 'academic'. Why can't I just use the internet?'

Academic publications are all **peer-reviewed**. This means that before an article or book is published, it is checked by other experts in the field to make sure that it's reliable, correct and of a high enough standard. This is why you know you can trust them.

Peer review The process by which academic work is assessed by other experts to judge whether or not it is of an acceptable standard to be published.

Look at the following sources. Are they okay to use in your work? Why/ Why not?

☐ Wikipedia article...Yes/No

....

....

☐ Academic journal article..Yes/No

....

....

☐ Newspaper article...Yes/No

....

....

☐ Book...Yes/No

....

....

How do I deal with counter arguments?

10 second
summary

Showing your awareness of other
points of view and demonstrating
their limitations will make your own
argument much stronger.

Arguments can only exist where there is more than one possible way of looking at things. A good argument is one that acknowledges other positions in order to demonstrate why its own answer is better, more convincing, or more useful for the current context.

In other words, counterarguments are not something to be frightened of, they are a vital part of making your own argument stronger. Sometimes giving proper consideration to a counterargument will also make you realise that it does have some validity, and lead you to modify your own thesis. This will make your argument more nuanced and convincing.

A student told us

'Coming up with different ways to argue about an issue is all part of the fun!'

Finding counterarguments

Once you have developed your own position, you can start to look for other points of view that might challenge your argument. Here are some places that you can look.

What your lecturer has told you

If you are answering a question set by your lecturer, they will have set it for a reason. Think about any debates or areas of disagreement they have mentioned, explicitly or implicitly, in their lectures, in class, or in course materials.

What you have read

Your lecturers will also have asked you to read things for a reason. Think about texts that are relevant to your argument, and even about ones that are not – they might seem irrelevant precisely because they are coming at the issue from another angle.

Different theoretical standpoints

Some arguments differ because the theoretical framework they've used has led to a different interpretation; a Marxist will argue differently from a neo-liberal, for example. Once you get more familiar with different theoretical standpoints in your own area you will be able both to identify these differences more easily, and make predictions about them yourself.

Historical/disciplinary developments

Ways of thinking about questions in any area of study change over time, for all sorts of reasons. Therefore *when* an argument was made might be as important as *what* is being argued. As with theoretical standpoints, the more familiar you become with your subject, the more you will learn about how thinking has changed over time.

Problematise the question

Sometimes the best way to think about other ways of responding is to check and see if there are any ways that you can show that the question itself is problematic.

For example, consider the presentation question we looked at in Section 5:

Equality is guaranteed by law in the UK – but has racial equality been achieved in reality?

One possible argument that you could make by problematising the terms of the question here is to say that equality has to be guaranteed by law in the UK *precisely because it has not been achieved in reality*. If it had, there would be no need for legislation.

Tip

A counterargument doesn't have to be a rejection of, or the complete opposite of, your argument. It could just be an alternative way of looking at an issue or question.

Generating counterarguments

As well as looking for counterarguments in the work of others, you should also see what you can come up with yourself, just by looking at the question.

Look at the following essay
question again

Feminism is the most important movement of the twentieth century. Discuss.

What counterarguments, or challenges, can you come up with to this statement? You can use points that you are aware of, but you don't necessarily have to have any knowledge about the question to do this.

Remember to problematise, if you can, and that any counterargument doesn't have to say that feminism was not important *at all*, just that it wasn't the *most* important.

Take five minutes to come up with as many points as you can.

....
....
....
....
....
....
....
....
....
....
....
....
....
....
....
....
....
....
....
....
....

Here are some examples. Some are stronger than others, and there are lots of other possibilities:

1   Another movement was more important (e.g. anti-colonialism, civil rights, trade unionism).

2   The goal of feminism was gender equality, which has not been achieved.

3   Feminism has not benefited all women, with progress primarily in Western societies.

4   It's impossible to compare different movements against each other, as they are so diverse.

5   Feminism is an umbrella term for a hugely diverse range of movements that are very difficult to discuss in generalised terms.

As you can see, some of these points require existing knowledge about the topic. However, point 1 definitely does not, it just uses the logic of the question, while points 4 and 5 also do not really require you to know anything to begin with. Points 4 and 5 are further examples of problematising the question.

Incorporating counterarguments

In order to incorporate counterarguments into your thinking, there are two things that you need to think about. First, you may need to modify your overall position. For example, look again at this thesis statement from Section 5.

This presentation will argue that <u>despite some improvements,</u> racial equality is still not a reality in the UK.

The underlined section shows where counterarguments have been considered, and some of their validity recognised. The overall argument is not weaker because of this, but stronger, as it has already shown that it rejects the notion that an improvement in equality is enough.

'If you're going to set up a counterargument, you need to make sure you knock it down afterwards.'

You also need to think about where counterarguments go in your own argument. You need to make sure that you've properly responded to the counterargument, so they should NEVER come last.

You have two options:

COUNTERARGUMENT → RESPONSE

For an example of this, see the 'block structure' example in Section 5.

or

ARGUMENT → COUNTERARGUMENT → IMPROVED ARGUMENT

For example:

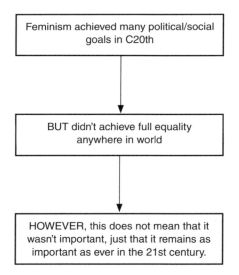

CHECK
POINT

Before you start producing your final argument, ask yourself the following questions.

Have you:

☐ Considered all possible challenges to your position?

☐ Considered how different theoretical standpoints might affect your argument?

☐ Thought about problematising the question?

If the answer to any of the above is 'no', then make sure to spend more time going through your notes. If the answer is 'yes', then you are ready for the next stage!

Congratulations!

You now have a full plan, and are ready to build your argument. By making sure to prepare properly, this should now be much easier, as you have already done the hard work of thinking everything through.

How do I write a good argument?

You've laid the foundations for your argument, and done all your preparation, but now you actually need to write it.

Throughout this section we will talk about 'writing', but what we discuss is relevant to constructing any sort of argument, including presentations and seminar discussions. Whatever you are producing, or even if you are just thinking about an issue and doing some research, it is very easy for your argument to get tangled and confused when you move from the planning stage to the actual *doing*.

One key thing to remember is to keep your overall destination in mind at all times throughout the process. As well as making sure that you are explaining individual points clearly, you need to step back regularly and make sure that your overall line of argument is driving straight towards the final goal.

Things to remember when writing an argument

1   Refer back to your plan regularly. It's fine to make changes as you go, but these must be **deliberate** changes.

2   Have you **signposted** your argument clearly? Make sure you have made it really clear to your reader how your points relate to each other, and what they mean.

3   Is everything in your argument **relevant** to your purpose, and **necessary** to your conclusion?

Signposting language is what we call anything you say to give your reader clear indicators of how points relate, and what they should be focusing on. This is not only about using words such as 'However', 'Nevertheless' or 'On the other hand', as while these connectors

> Signposting language What you say to give your reader clear indicators of how points relate, and what they should be focusing on.

can be useful, many students overuse them. You do not need to use any special language to signpost, just think about how to make it clear to your reader that you are moving to a different point of view, or that something is important, and so on.

Keep this in mind while you are reading this book, and you will start to see lots of examples.

A student told us

'I don't know what academic style is, and don't think my writing is good enough for university.'

Writing well at university is often overcomplicated, and many students are intimidated when they don't need to be. There is no such thing as one good 'academic style', as the language that you need to use differs depending on what subject you are writing about, what task you are undertaking, and what you are trying to achieve. Rather than getting bogged down worrying about grammar and style when building an argument, then, it's much more important to think about what you are doing and why – and how your language can help you achieve what you want it to.

ACTIVITY Reflect on your subject area

Take a few minutes to think about the following questions, and note down your thoughts below:

- What is a 'good argument' in your subject?
- What evidence are you using?
- What are you trying to achieve?

....

....

....

....

....

....

....

....

What is a 'good argument' in your subject?

Different subjects are looking for different types of argument, and different tasks require different arguments as well. Literature and philosophy essays involve different styles of argument, for example, while the skills involved in working out a research question from a gap in the literature is very different from analysing whether your research has filled that gap.

The more study you do, and the more you read, the more you will learn about how to argue within the context of your discipline.

What evidence are you using?

In literature, for example, your raw material could be poetry, or fiction, whereas in sociology, it could be the outcomes of a series of interviews, or survey data. How does what you are arguing with/about change what comes out the other end?

What are you trying to achieve?

Sometimes this will be very clear, as you will have been set a question and given specific instructions – but whatever you are doing, it's very important to think about your end goal. Are you trying to explain, for example, what something means? Or how something happened? Or what therapy is best for a particular problem? Or how some new evidence changes the existing paradigm? They will all require different types of argument.

> 'Knowing exactly what impact you want your argument to have is a vital step in making it successful.'

Reviewing and redrafting

Reviewing and redrafting your work is one of the most important parts of building a good argument. No matter how well you have prepared, there will always be mistakes to correct, and things that could have been done better.

Three top tips

1   **Think like a reader**. If you were reading what you had written would it make sense to you?

2   **Re-drafting is different from proofreading**. Think about the overall argument and the order your points are in, as well as just looking for mistakes.

3   **If something feels wrong – change it**. Don't just gloss over it and move on.

Presenting an argument verbally

- Make sure to **practise** at least once. Read it out loud! As a rule of thumb, 1000 words takes around ten minutes to present, but you need to know how fast you actually go when you're under pressure.

- Remember that you are writing to be **heard**, not to be read – some things that look okay written down sound terrible when you say them out loud.

- **Signposting** and **repetition** are vital. Make sure your audience can clearly understand how all your points relate to each other, and repeat the important points so that they know exactly what your argument is.

CHECK POINT

Do you:

☐ Understand what your subject means by a 'good argument'?

☐ Know what evidence you are expected to use, and how this affects your argument?

If the answer to either of the above is 'no', ask one of your tutors, or a fellow student. Also, remember that you can learn a lot about both these questions when reading for your studies – so make sure that when you are reading, you think like a writer!

What makes a killer conclusion?

10 second
summary

Your conclusion is the place where
you can make it absolutely clear to
your reader what they should be
taking away from your work.

Writing a good conclusion is one of the most important elements in making sure your argument has the most impact – and gets the best marks. Your reader should have absolutely no doubt over what you are trying to argue, and a good argument should be simple to understand, even if it deals with very complex matters. Your conclusion is the last thing they will read, and it is your chance to make sure you've got your message across.

You shouldn't be introducing new ideas in a conclusion – but that doesn't mean you need to just repeat everything you've said. This is your chance to highlight your key points, reiterate the most important stages, and leave your reader securely at their destination: the answer.

What should a conclusion do?

Your conclusion must:

- Review and highlight your key points

- Give a clear and complete answer to the question

- Bring your argument to a close – you can signal areas that are not fully resolved, but you must have made your point. Otherwise, you have not answered the question.

Your conclusion must not:

- Be undecided, or duck the question – you can say that a question is very complex, but a woolly answer that says something like 'there are so many factors it is difficult to say' is not acceptable

- Be based on anything other than evidence and reason

- Just repeat what has been said in the main body.

A student told us

'I hate writing conclusions, I never know how to wrap things up.'

Writing your conclusion

The good news is that writing a killer conclusion is all about the planning. The work that you put in analysing your question, generating ideas and writing a thesis statement pay off at this point – because you know exactly what you want to say.

As an example, let's go back to the presentation question that we looked at earlier:

Question: *Equality is guaranteed by law in the UK – but has racial equality been achieved in reality?*

Thesis statement: *Despite some improvements, racial equality is still not a reality in the UK.*

Remember that we also talked about problematising the question, and arguing that equality has to be guaranteed by law in the UK precisely because it has not been achieved in reality.

In Section 5 we looked at examples of how a response to this question could have been structured.

Here is one to remind you:

YES:

- Racial equality protected by law (1)
- More prominent people of colour across many areas of UK culture and society (5)
- Current UK government most ethnically diverse ever, with c.10% BAME MPs (2).

HOWEVER

NO:

- 14% UK population from an ethnic minority background (6) = parliament still not representative
- Business the same → only 7.4% BAME board members (4)
- 26% admit prejudice (3)
- Brexit vote → increasing no. racist attacks (7).

What would you write in the conclusion, based on all of the above? See if you can write it in 100 words:

....

....

....

....

....

....

....

....

Example conclusion

It is clear, then, that while there have been some improvements in racial equality in the UK, it is by no means yet a reality. Despite a historically diverse parliament, and an increasing number of prominent social and cultural figures being people of colour, there is no sphere in which representation yet matches the population of the country, whether that be business, politics or education, where attainment gaps remain a huge issue. In fact, it could be argued that the very fact that new legislation aimed at tackling inequalities, including racial inequalities, was needed as recently as 2010 is a sign of the continuing scale of the problem, not of its disappearance.

This is just one example: there is no one right way to do this.

Note how:

- This example takes language directly from the thesis statement, and the question. This helps to make the answer to the question absolutely clear
- If the thesis statement was given in the introduction, this also helps to bring things full circle and make the argument feel complete
- The main points are touched on, but no great detail is needed as this will already have been given elsewhere.

Concluding a presentation

If you are delivering your argument verbally rather than in text form, it is important to remember that your audience will need more help. It's different to listen, than to read: you can't go at your own pace, or go back and re-read something that you weren't sure about.

That means that when concluding, you need to:

- Use simple and clear language
- Repeat the question and the key points of your argument, and deliver them in short sentences wherever possible. Short sentences are easier to understand, and to follow
- Be explicit about your answer.

For example: *'I have been talking to you about whether or not racial equality has been achieved in the UK. The answer is clearly no. There have been some improvements, but there are still clear inequalities. People from ethnic minority backgrounds in the UK are not represented fairly in politics, in business, or in education – or anywhere. The 2010 legislation needs to be seen as a tool to try and make racial equality a reality, not a sign that it already is.'*

Answers:

1   No. Your conclusion is a review of your argument, not a repetition of it.

2   No. If something is important enough to be in your conclusion, it should have been mentioned in the main body of the argument.

3   Yes. This is your chance to make sure your audience fully understands your position. Make it count.

4   No. Your conclusion should make your position clear, but this is about rational argument, not opinion.

CHECK POINT

Considering the features of a conclusion, circle the correct answers below.

A conclusion should:

1   Repeat all your main points. .... yes/no

2   Introduce new ideas. .... yes/no

3   Be clear and concise. .... yes/no

4   Give your opinion. .... yes/no

How do I do better next time?

10 second summary

The only way to get better at anything is to make sure you learn from what you have done before.

Every time you build an argument, you should reflect on your experience to see how you can do better next time. This means thinking honestly about what went well and what didn't, and setting yourself practical and achievable goals for next time.

Whether you are looking backwards or forwards, don't try to tackle everything all in one go. If you try and think about the whole task that you just completed, it can be overwhelming. Equally, if you just say, 'Next time I will do better', without thinking about exactly how, then you will end up just repeating the same process.

A student told us

'I don't have time to stop and think about the work I just handed in – I'm straight on to the next assignment!'

University is very busy, and so is your life, and it's easy to feel overwhelmed by all the things that you need to do. But making time to stop and think is really important – it will help you not only get better at all the skills you need to master, it will also help you to keep focused on your studies as a whole, on how everything fits together, and where it can take you.

Setting goals

In order to set yourself useful goals for next time, it is important to:

- **Focus on the positives as well as the negatives**. If you only think about what went wrong then you will place too much emphasis on that, and demoralise yourself. It's really important to give yourself credit, and to recognise what you do well so that you can do it again in the future, and build on it.

- **Set manageable, practical goals**. You have to set yourself tasks that you can actually achieve, and that are realistic. 'I will write better arguments' will not get you anywhere as it's too big, and too vague. Likewise, 'I will get a first next time' is an admirable goal, but not entirely in your control. 'I will spend more time planning my next presentation', on the other hand, is measurable and achievable, and something you can actually **do**.

Let's reflect on what you've done while reading this book. If you've been using it to help you with an assignment or specific task, then think about how that has gone. If you've been reading it as a general aid, then think about your experience with building arguments in your studies up until now.

Think about each stage of the process. For each stage, write at least one thing that you did/do well (a positive) and one thing that you could have done/do better (a negative) in the table.

	What went well	What I could do better
1 Analysing the question and understanding my purpose		
2 Generating ideas and reviewing what I've learnt		
3 Doing extra research and finding new evidence		
4 Identifying, generating and incorporating counterarguments		
5 Writing a clear thesis statement		
6 Building a structure and working out what to include		
7 Writing a clear argument		
8 Reviewing and redrafting		

If you can, narrow this down to a list of three things that you do well, and three things that you need to improve on.

Things I do well

1 ....

2 ....

3 ....

Things I need to improve on

1 ....

2 ....

3 ....

Now, set yourself three practical and achievable goals for the next time you build an argument. These can either be in response to the things that you need to improve on, or a way of building on what went well.

Goals for next time

1 ....

2 ....

3 ....

If you carry out this process regularly throughout your studies, you'll find that you will get much better at learning from your mistakes, and getting even better at your strengths.

CHECK POINT

Last but not least, pick three ideas, or tips, from this book that you have found particularly useful, and that you are going to make sure to use in future.

1 ....

....

....

2 ....

....

....

3 ....

....

....

Final checklist

To be absolutely sure you know how to build a good argument, work through this final checklist.

I understand what an argument is in an academic context. ❏

I've thought about why my lecturers set the tasks they do, and how they relate to my studies. ❏

I understand how different types of argument relate to different tasks. ❏

I know how to come up with ideas and different possible answers. ❏

I know how to structure my argument and prepare a detailed plan. ❏

I know how to support my argument with evidence. ❏

I know how to decide if I can trust a source or not. ❏

I know how to find, generate and incorporate counterarguments. ❏

I know how to come up with a strong conclusion. ❏

I've thought about what I can do better next time. ❏

Glossary

Block structure   A way of structuring your argument so that different positions, or sides are dealt with in 'blocks'.

Confirmation bias   The tendency to focus on things that confirm our existing ideas, and discount what challenges them.

Discursive argument   An argument that discusses the different possible ways of looking at a question or issue.

Explanatory argument   An argument that explains things: for example, *why* something is the way it is, *how* something works, or *what* would happen in different scenarios.

Peer review   The process by which academic work is assessed by other experts to judge whether or not it is of an acceptable standard to be published.

Point by point structure   A way of structuring your argument so that points are grouped thematically.

Synthesis   Bringing together different views in order to form an overall position that combines them all.

Signposting language   What you say to give your reader clear indicators of how points relate, and what they should be focusing on.

Thesis statement   A short summary of exactly what your argument is about. Basically, this is your answer in a nutshell.

Further reading and resources

The **Purdue Online Writing Lab (or OWL)** at owl.purdue.edu/owl/purdue_owl.html has a huge range of resources to help students with writing for university. Search 'argument' in the site's search function to find a wealth of excellent material on how to organise and structure arguments.

The **Royal Literary Fund** runs a fellowship scheme where professional writers use their expertise to help students write well at university. They have some excellent advice on building arguments at https://www.rlf.org.uk/resources/are-you-looking-for-an-argument/.

The **Open University** also offers a range of study skills material for free at https://help.open.ac.uk/topic/study-skills, including lots of material on how to build a good argument.

Thomas, F-N. and Turner, M. (2011) *Clear and Simple as the Truth*. 2nd Edition. Princeton & Oxford, Princeton University Press is a very useful discussion of how to write well, particularly in terms of thinking about your purpose and writing style.

Online whiteboard apps such as **Padlet** can be really useful for note-taking, planning and collaborating with others.

Also remember to familiarise yourself with all the **support available at your own university**, whether that be from your **own department and lecturers**, the **library**, **skills support teams**, or **online**.